Powerful Ideas in the Classroom

Using Squeak to Enhance Math and Science Learning

B.J. Allen-Conn & Kim Rose

Afterword by Alan Kay

Many of the designations used by companies to distinguish their products are often claimed as trademarks or registered trademarks. In all instances where the authors are aware of a claim, the product names appear in italics. Readers, however, should contact the appropriate companies for more complete information regarding trademarks, registration and product details.

⚠ BE CAREFUL! The activities and projects in this work were designed with safety and success in mind. But even the simplest activity or the most common materials could be harmful when mishandled or misused. Use common sense whenever you're exploring or experimenting.

Cover art by Peter Maguire.

This book was prepared using the LaTeX document preparation system and reproduced by Typecraft Wood & Jones from final *PDF* files supplied by the authors.
www.typecraft.com

Printed in the United States of America.

Published by Viewpoints Research Institute, Inc., Glendale, California.
www.viewpointsresearch.org

The publication of this book was funded in part by the National Science Foundation under Grant No. 0228806. Opinions expressed are those of the authors and do not necessarily reflect those of the Foundation.

ISBN 0–9743131–0–6

11 10 9 8 7 6 5 4 3 2 1

Contents

"What is a powerful idea?" "To what domain of life or learning are you referring?" We were confronted with these questions by a colleague upon her review of an early draft of this project book.

To begin a discussion of "powerful ideas" we need to give a deep and humble bow to both Seymour Papert and Alan Kay. Papert — a renowned educator, mathematician, computer scientist and creator of the Logo programming language — first discussed "powerful ideas" in his book *Mindstorms: Children, Computers and Powerful Ideas*. What did Seymour mean by a "powerful idea?" He defined a "powerful idea" as an "intellectual tool." Seymour believed that exploring powerful ideas through the use of computers, as well as off-computer activities, could give children a way to confront their intuitions. He believed that computers could help children by allowing them to externalize their intuitive expectations, and by using computational materials such as simulations and models they might be able to reconsider or remodel their intuitive knowledge.

Alan Kay — our friend, mentor, leader and driving force behind Squeak — was deeply influenced by Seymour and his ideas. It was Seymour's ideas that provoked and drew the idea of the "Dynabook" from Alan, and began a quest to create dynamic tools for children to amplify their learning that has now spanned over 30 years. Alan has guided us over the last several years and together we have developed this sequence of projects which sits upon a foundation of Seymour's and Alan's ideas.

In our work with children we have found many cases where their intuitive belief systems are in direct conflict with how something really works — simple things like balls being dropped from the classroom roof, for example. A child's intuitive belief is often that a twelve pound shotput will hit the ground before a foam ball. After experiencing a number of outdoor activities, including watching various balls drop and even timing them, some children learn this is not the case; others hold strong and steadfast to their initial beliefs. After further investigation with the aid of computer models and simulations that the children create themselves, children can see conflict with their intuitions and in the end are rewarded with a great "aha!" — a powerful idea about how their world works that they can now internalize and deeply understand.

This book was written to share several project ideas that can be used inside or outside the classroom. It will investigate a number of powerful ideas through projects that children create in Squeak and via tangential activities we call "excursions." Excursions either introduce powerful ideas that can be explored within Squeak or they illustrate key concepts from another perspective, through non-computer-based, hands-on activities. This book is intended to be a starting point for understanding how Squeak projects can be created to amplify learning experiences and activities.

The projects in this book explore powerful ideas in mathematics and science such as zero, positive and negative numbers, x and y coordinates, ratio, feedback, acceleration and gravity. A variable can be considered a powerful idea in the area of computer programming. Powerful teaching methodologies include collaborative working, mentoring and articulating student understanding through a variety of media.

The basis for exploring these ideas is a series of projects starting with making your own car. We know that every kid wants to "drive a car." The projects build on each other and on the concepts they introduce. It is assumed that mathematics instruction will be given prior to, or in conjunction with, the projects in this book. In addition, we believe that using multiple media (books, the Internet, video, etc.) helps learners gain understanding and multiple points of view.

Squeak is much more than a word processor — it is an *idea processor*. It is a language, a tool and a media authoring environment. If you don't already have Squeak, you can download it from the Squeakland web site (`http://www.squeakland.org`). Squeak is free (really!) and runs on all major computer platforms. It is the result of an open source effort under the umbrella of Viewpoints Research Institute, Inc., a non-profit organization (http://www.viewpointsresearch.org/about.html).

Ideally, before using this book, you should install Squeak on your computer and complete the introductory online tutorials which can be found on the Squeakland site at http://www.squeakland.org/author/etoys.html.

Squeak is a "deep" system and has different entry points for different kinds of users. The projects in this book are all based in the entry-level "Etoy" component of Squeak. This can be found and downloaded from the Squeakland.org website. "Etoys" ("Electronic," "Educational," "Exciting," "Exploratory") are models, simulations and games constructed by assembling tiles into scripts which send commands to painted objects intended to give a learner insight into an area of investigation. Later, as users become more adept at creating such scripts, they can move into other areas of Squeak's interface more suitable for their learning level. Expert users of Squeak (professional computer programmers and media developers) would not use the Etoy component for their creations, but a more expert level offering a different "look and feel" and extended facilities.

We invite you to join the Squeakland community online by subscribing to the mailing list (http://www.squeakland.org/join). We encourage you to share your project ideas and examples. The projects contained in this book are based on a few powerful ideas. It is our dream to initiate the creation of "a thousand pieces of content" and have them shared via the Internet, CD-ROMs and books. We hope you will add to this body of knowledge and help us to develop both Squeak and its accompanying curricula.

We hope that you will have fun with these projects and that they will unlock some powerful ideas for you and your children. Finally, we give our profound thanks to Alan and Seymour for their ideas and passion, and for the inspiration they have given us to continue exploring how computers can help children understand powerful ideas.

BJ Allen-Conn,   Los Angeles, California
Kim Rose   July 2003

Project 1

Etoy Basics
and
Painting the Car

The first part of this project is presented as narrative and is intended to teach some fundamentals of the Etoy system. Etoys are created in a "World." The unit saved — or "published" — is a "Project." Painted sketches, when kept, become "objects."

The second part of Project 1 asks learners to paint their first object, a car. Through painting the car learners will become familiar with the Etoy paint tools. Painting the car as seen from above is important to the understanding of the next several projects.

About the Book's Format

At the beginning of each project this column will introduce:

Project Prerequisites: Squeak

- The specific tools or parts of the Etoy system needed to complete the project.

Related Math Concepts

- Any specific math or science concepts the project illustrates.

  These concepts will often correspond to the national guidelines and state frameworks.

Curricular Objectives

- The intended goals and outcomes for the learner.

Open Squeak's Etoy component by clicking on the Squeak shortcut (or alias) that was created on your desktop after you downloaded it from the Internet.

You will see a blank screen containing two flaps — Navigator and Supplies.

This screen is a "World" in which to create, explore and learn! It is within this "World" that you will construct the projects in this book.

Projects created within the World can be assembled using a variety of media types such as paintings and drawings, text, video and photographs (jpegs or bmps). The projects in this book primarily use paintings (or "sketches") created with Squeak's paint tools. The paint tools can be revealed by clicking the "brush" button found in the orange Navigator flap at the bottom of the screen.

The paint tools are used to create *sketches* that, once kept, will be transformed into *objects*. These objects can be *scripted* to behave as you desire.

It is projects that are saved, or "published," in Squeak. Projects can be published to your local hard disk, to a classroom or home server, or to the Internet. The commands for Publishing can be found in the Navigator flap. If you hold down the **Publish It!** button on the Navigator you will see the options for saving projects. When first selecting a publishing option, you will be prompted to give the project a name. Once published the project will be saved on your local disk in the "My Squeak" folder, as a file ending with ".pr" (indicating that the file is a Squeak project).

This project is the first of several that will feature a small car. Open Squeak. Bring up the paint tools by opening the Navigator flap and then click on the brush.

This column on project pages will introduce:

 Select a nice color and use the largest paint brush size to paint an oval. This will be the car's body.

Challenges

 Select a smaller brush size and paint the tires.

- Suggested challenges that are intended to extend thinking and the use of the concepts and objectives for the project.

 Select the color white and paint a small windshield. Finally, paint the car's headlights. Use a different color than the one used to paint the car.

Notes

When you are happy with the painting, click the **Keep** button. This will transform the painting into an object and hide the paint tools.

- Related notes that are intended for a teacher, parent or mentor.

Place the cursor over the center of the car and wait a moment for its *handles* (object "controls") to appear. Clicking on any single handle will *reveal* them fully. (Alt-click on Windows, or Command-click on Macs, will also fully reveal any object's handles.)

car

The green arrow positioned in the center of the object indicates the direction in which it will move forward. To change the direction, click on the arrow and drag it in the direction you want the car to move forward.

To name the car, click on the word "sketch" to highlight it and type a new name. Click on return (or enter) to accept the name change. The next step is to save the car as a completed project.

When you downloaded Squeak onto your computer, a folder was created on the desktop called MySqueak. This is where saved projects will be stored. To get a project into this folder, click on the Navigator flap and MouseDown on the **Publish It!** button. The dialog box to the right will appear.

MySqueak

Name the project. Once you have named it, click on the **OK** button found in the box. When the blue publish window appears, click on MySqueak to highlight it and then click on **Save**. Your project will be saved in the MySqueak folder located on your computer's desktop.

Now that the project is saved you can quit Squeak by clicking the **QUIT** button on the Navigator.

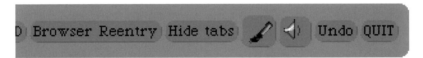

Loading Projects

When you want to load a project back into Squeak, open the Navigator flap and click the **Find** button.

When the blue window appears, select MySqueak. All of your saved projects will appear in the window on the right. Select the project you want to open by clicking and highlighting it, then click the **OK** button. This will load the selected project into Squeak.

Project 2

Playing with the Car

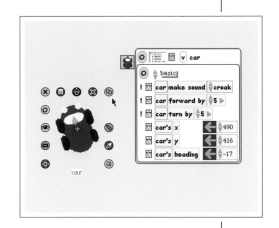

In this project learners will explore the manipulation and change of characteristics or behaviors of their object (the car) by changing its values and settings in the world and in its viewer.

The painted object presents the learner with an iconic representation. The object's viewer reveals the object's characteristics (its location in the world, heading, size and color) through a symbolic representation (by showing numeric values). The "Montessori game" here is for children to get their pay-off playing in the hand-eye arena, while gradually and subliminally gaining fluency in and an appreciation for the power of symbols.

For children to realize that their car's "heading" is a number is a powerful idea. To see the car's location in the world also as numbers is powerful. Through exploration and play they will see how each value can be postive, negative, or zero.

Exploration can be extended by using the "PenDown" feature of an object. Geometric shapes can be made by an object's pen by creating scripts with just the "forward by" and "turn by" tiles.

This initial exploration is critical to set the foundation for further play and for the creation of subsequent Etoy projects.

Project Prerequisites: Squeak

- Painting.

- Naming objects.

- Setting the forward direction of an object.

- Revealing an object's viewer.

- Saving a project.

Related Math Concepts

- The concept of "x" and "y" coordinates.

- The concept of positive and negative numbers.

- Headings as angles and the number of degrees in a circle.

Curricular Objectives

- Understanding coordinate systems.

- Providing a foundation for the understanding of simple geometric shapes and angles.

In this project you will explore your painted car as an object. If you have saved your car as a project you should load that project now. If you didn't save your car you need to paint a new car for this project.

MouseOver the car or click on the object while selecting the Command (Mac) or Alt (Windows) key to reveal its handles. If you let the mouse linger over any handle for a moment, you will see it is equipped with balloon help to remind you of its purpose. The figure below shows the car with all its handles and a description of what each handle does.

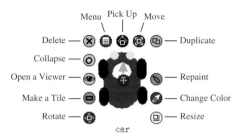

Click on the turquoise "eyeball" handle to reveal the object's viewer. The viewer below shows the "basic" category. Additional categories can be revealed by clicking on the category name or by clicking on the up or down arrowhead to the left of any category name.

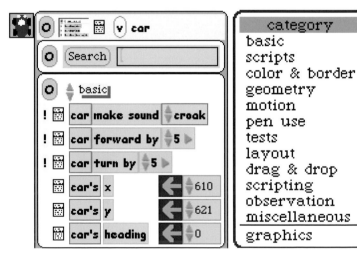

MouseDown on the blue "rotation" handle of the car and move it to the left and right. Notice the value changing in the "car's heading" tiles in the viewer.

Pick up the car and move it around the world. Notice the changes in the "car's x" and "car's y" value tiles.

Look at the tiles in the **basic** category pane. You'll see two types of tile; some are preceded by a yellow exclamation point and others are not. The tiles following an exclamation point are *action tiles*.

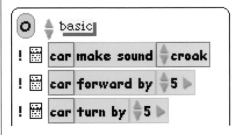

Clicking on an exclamation point will "fire" the action once. Holding down an exclamation point will "run" the action repeatedly. Try driving the car "around the world" using the exclamation points.

Numeric values of the tiles can be changed by either clicking on the up or down arrowhead to the left of the value, or by selecting the current value, typing in a new number and hitting return (or enter). Play around with these numbers and use the exclamation point to continue to explore.

What happens to your object if you make the value of the "forward by" tile a negative number and then click or hold down the exclamation point? Explore and experiment!

Tiles which are not followed by an exclamation point are "value" tiles. Each of these is followed by a green arrow that assigns or sets that value (a placeholder for any number) as the current value for the particular attribute or property of that object at a given time. Change the values of these tiles and notice what happens to the car.

Scripts are created for objects by assembling tiles. To get a Scriptor (a "**script** edit**or**") drag the "Car emptyScript" tiles (or "Sketch" if you haven't named your car) from the **scripts** category onto the World. If the **scripts** category is not visible in your object's viewer, reveal it now (as explained earlier).

Scriptor

To create a script, add the "Car forward by 5" tiles to the scriptor by dragging and dropping them into the empty scriptor. When a script is ready to "accept" tiles, a bright green rectangle will appear indicating it is okay to add tiles to the scriptor.

Note: The cursor *must* be in the scriptor for it to accept tiles. If the tile graphic is in the scriptor, but the cursor is not, the tiles will not be accepted into the script.

Script

Any string of action tiles (those preceeded by an exclamation point) will create their own scriptor when dragged and dropped onto the World. Value tiles must be added to a scriptor or to a string of tiles already in a scriptor. They will not create their own scriptor when dragged and dropped onto the world.

Misplaced tiles can be deleted in two ways: by dragging them into the trash (found in the Supplies flap) or by bringing up their handles and clicking on the "delete" ⊗ handle. Once tiles have been joined they cannot be disconnected. If you accidentally make a string of tiles or if you find you have tiles you no longer need, throw them in the trash.

Trash

Scripts can be run (or "activated") by clicking on the small clock in the scriptor or by selecting the "normal" button and changing its setting to "ticking." To fire (or "step") a script, click on the exclamation point.

Clock

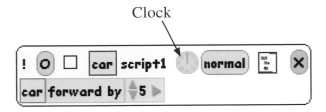

What can you add to this script that will make the car go forward and turn simultaneously?

Pen trails can be set for any object so that its movement in the world can be visualized. Reveal the **pen use** category in the car's viewer. Change the car's "penDown" value to "true" and set the script to "ticking." Notice the trail left by the car. The pen size can be changed by increasing its numeric value. The pen color can also be changed.

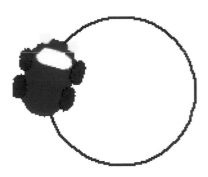

Once a project contains multiple scripts it is wise to get a set of "stop step go" buttons from the Supplies flap and place it on the World. Clicking **go** will set all of your project's scripts ticking. Clicking **stop** will pause all scripts.

Challenge

- Explore to discover how many geometric shapes can be created by making simple scripts for the car.

Project 3

Controlling the Car with a Steering Wheel

In this project learners will create two objects and make them interact. Prior to this they've been manipulating a single object with an accompanying script. In this project learners will have to take tiles from one object (the steering wheel) and add them to another object's (the car's) script. This requires an escalation in the learner's thinking and may take a little more time for some.

This project requires creating an Etoy with multiple objects, as well as creating scripts for those objects. Some scripts will contain properties from two objects. This project also requires the learner to switch from one object's viewer to another and to think about multiple viewers within a project.

Once this project is completed learners can be challenged to create other projects using multiple objects with similar scripts. At this point children often change their objects from cars to animals, airplanes or other small figures as they discover that Squeak's capabilities are as broad as their imaginations.

Project Prerequisites: Squeak

- Painting.

- Naming objects.

- Setting an object's forward direction.

- Creating scripts.

Related Math Concepts

- The concept of positive and negative numbers.

- The concept of heading.

Curricular Objectives

- Understanding how the turn of the car relates to the heading of the steering wheel.

- Understanding how numeric feedback from the steering wheel's heading can help steer the car.

- Understanding how textual tiles are representations of values.

- Forming hypotheses based on findings to make predictions.

In this project you will learn how to drive the car with a steering wheel.

Paint a car and a steering wheel. These objects must be painted separately. An example of each is shown above. Name both the car and the wheel.

The goal of the lesson is to use the concept of positive and negative numbers (as on a number line) to help steer the car. To do this you will need to connect the car and the steering wheel together. The car will be the scripted object.

Open the car's viewer to reveal its tiles and drag the "forward by" tiles onto the world. Drag the "turn by" tiles and place them below the "forward by" tiles in the same script.

Bring up the handles for the steering wheel and reveal its tiles by clicking on the turquoise "eyeball" 👁 handle. Click and hold the blue "rotation" handle of the steering wheel to turn the wheel to the right and to the left. Look at the viewer and notice what is happening to the numeric value of the steering wheel's heading as you rotate the wheel.

Blue Rotation Handle ⟶

Wheel

It is important to understand that once the two objects are connected together and the heading of the steering wheel is indicating zero, the car will go straight. When the heading of the steering wheel indicates a negative number, the car will turn to the left; when the heading of the steering wheel indicates a positive number, the car will turn to the right.

The next step is to connect the turn of the car to the heading of the steering wheel. This is done by dragging the "heading" tiles of the steering wheel and placing them on the *value* of the "turn by" tiles of the car.

When the script is created, you are ready to drive the car. In the steering wheel's **basic** category, set the value of the steering wheel's "heading" to 0. Start the script and quickly bring up the handles of the steering wheel. MouseDown on the blue "rotation" handle and begin steering the car.

Once the two objects are connected and you move the steering wheel to the right and to the left using its blue "rotation" handle, the car will respond and turn in the same direction.

If you are having difficulty with the car's directional turns, visualize yourself as the driver inside the car. You may need to slow down the car by changing the value of the "forward by" tiles. A *detailed watcher* is another tool in Squeak that can help. To get a detailed watcher, click on the tiny menu found to the left of the "wheel's heading" tiles.

Select "detailed watcher". Place the watcher on the world. Now, as you steer the car, use the watcher's changing value as a guide. Remember, a zero value for the heading means the car will go straight. Have fun driving!!!

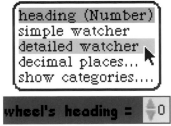

Wheel

Blue Rotation Handle

Challenge

- Build an obstacle course. Succesfully steer the car through the course without touching any of the obstacles. Use pen trails to mark the car's path.

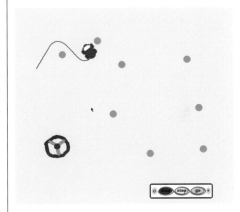

- Earn yourself a "Squeak Driver's License."

Project 4

Creating a "Smart" Car that Drives Itself Along a Road

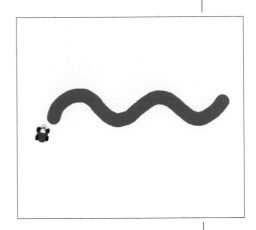

In this project learners will create a robotic car scripted to drive along a single-colored road using a painted sensor. This introduces the powerful idea of feedback and the use of conditional statements.

As in Project 3, learners must think about the car's heading and direction and the use of positive and negative numbers to control the car's turn. The car will follow a script using a conditional (if/then) statement "testing" what color the car "sees" using its painted sensor.

Sounds can be added to these projects providing another dimension of feedback. Sounds might indicate when the vehicle has driven off the road or when it has encountered an obstacle.

Exploring feedback is a great way to bridge the mechanical world and the world of biology. A variety of Etoys can be created based on this model of feedback for the exploration of ant, fish or other animal behaviors.

Project Prerequisites: Squeak

- Using test (Yes/No) tiles.

- Category in Viewer: **tests**.

Related Math Concepts

- Simple conditional statements.

- Using positive and negative numbers to control directionality.

Curricular Objectives

- Understanding how the turn of the road relates to the turn of the car.

- Using feedback from a sensor to keep the car following the road.

The aim of this project is to "program" a car to sense the road and steer itself along the road without using a steering wheel.

The object of the lesson is to use a single-colored sensor to create feedback. This example uses a yellow sensor placed at the front of the car.

 ← **Sensor**

Feedback will be used to determine the direction in which the car will need to turn in order to correct its heading and follow the road. This project requires a transfer of learning from the previous projects about positive and negative numbers. When the car veers to the left it will need to correct its turn by using a positive number, and if it veers to the right it will need to correct its turn by using a negative number.

This behavior is created by introducing a *test tile* (or "conditional statement") into the car's script. To find a test tile, click on the small beige icon found at the top of the scriptor.

Clicking on this icon will tear off a "Test/Yes/No" tile that can be added into the script. The next step is to give the sensor its instructions.

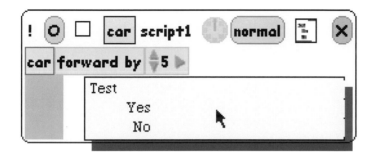

Find the **tests** category in the car's viewer. Select the "color sees" tiles from this category.

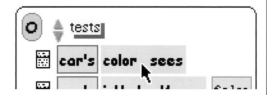

Drag these tiles into the script and place them next to the word "Test".

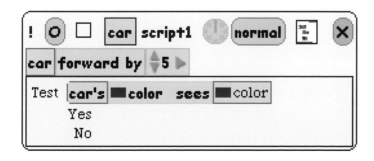

We want the color of the car's sensor to "see" the color of the road. Click on the first color rectangle and drag the eye-dropper over the sensor and MouseDown. The rectangle will change to the exact color of the sensor. Click on the second rectangle following the word "sees" and drag the eyedropper over the road to select its color.

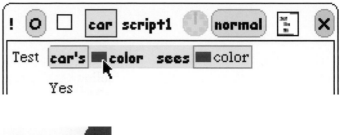

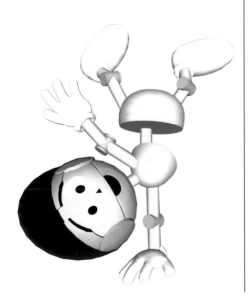

To complete the test we must determine which direction the car will need to turn in order to follow the road. The car's turn depends on whether it has been placed to the right of the road or to its left.

In this example the car was placed just to the left of the road.

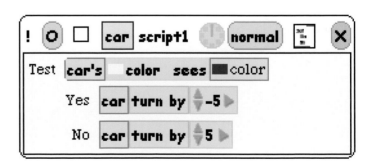

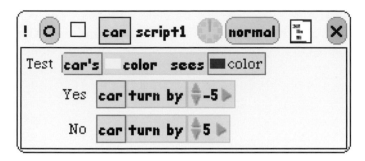

Challenges

Start the script by clicking on the clock or by setting the **paused** button to "ticking." Is the car following the road? If not, play with the values in the "turn by" tiles until it does.

There is more than one way to solve this problem. There are other ways to do a "color sees" test that can involve different parts of the car being used as sensors. Can you think of other ways to make a robotic car?

- Using what you have learned, script a car or some other object so it can successfully navigate a maze.

- Paint a second car. Place both cars on a road with two lanes of different colors. Can you make them travel side-by-side along the road and stay in their own lane?

You may have to make your road a bit larger or make your cars smaller. Both of these can be done by using the object's yellow "resize" handle.

What else will you need to think about in order to meet this challenge?

Boy!
This takes some *real* thinking!!!

Project 5

Racing Two Cars with Variable Speeds

This is the first project in which variables are created and used. The concept of "random" is introduced and random values are assigned to each car's speed.

As learners create multiple cars and assign random values to their speeds they can begin to think about a particular car's average speed, the mode speed and the median value as they simulate races between their cars and graph or plot the results.

This project sets a foundation for deeper thinking about this thing called "speed." In addition it introduces the concepts of constant versus accelerated motion, rate and the rate of change.

Project Prerequisites: Squeak

- Use of "test" tiles.

- Use of "color sees" tiles.

- Category in viewer: **scripting**.

- Naming scripts.

- Using a "detailed watcher".

Related Math Concepts

- Understanding variables and how to create and use them.

- Understanding the concept of "random" as it applies to numbers.

- Understanding the concepts of "mean," "mode," and "median."

- Using a line plot.

Curricular Objectives

- Creating a variable whose value is a random number.

- Using line plots to record the speed of a car.

- Using the information recorded on a line plot to determine the mean and mode of a car's speed.

- Forming hypotheses based on findings to make predictions.

What is a variable? A variable is something that has no fixed value and can assume any set of values. Variables can affect the outcome of an event. An object's speed is a variable, as is its length and its x or y coordinate in the World. In order to create a variable you need to create an object.

Start by painting a car and naming it.

To create a variable for the car, click on the "v" button found

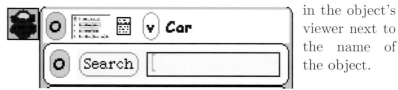

in the object's viewer next to the name of the object.

Name the variable "speed" and click the **Accept** button. This will create the variable and add it to your object's viewer

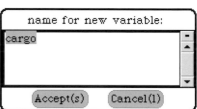

Drag the green assignment arrow onto the World. This will create a script for the car's variable "speed" tile.

When the script is created, click on the name of your object. The menu shown to the right will appear. Select "hand me a random number tile". A random number tile can also be found in the Supplies flap.

```
            script2
show code textually
save this version
destroy this script
rename this script
button to fire this script
edit balloon help for this script
fires per tick...
explain status alternatives
hand me a tile for self
hand me a "random number" tile
hand me a "button down?" tile
hand me a "button up?" tile
```

Replace the value of "speed" in the script with the "random" tile. Change the random number to a number less than 20.

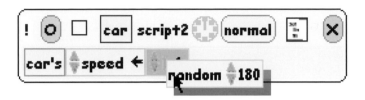

Note

- The remaining Etoy projects in this book will use variables.

To make the car go forward by its speed, drag the "car's speed" tiles and *replace the value of the car's "forward by" tile with the speed tiles.*

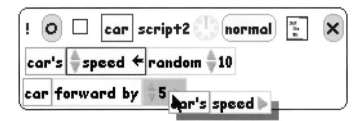

With each tick of the clock, the car will go forward any number of pixels from 1 to the maximum of your random number. To watch this as it changes, get a "detailed watcher." The watcher will show the number of pixels the car is moving forward with each tick of the clock.

Next to the "speed" variable in the **variables** category is an icon that looks like a tiny menu. Click on it and select "detailed watcher" from the menu. Place this watcher anywhere on the World.

Click on the exclamation point **!** in the script to fire it once. What does the detailed watcher report as the car's speed? Do this several times.

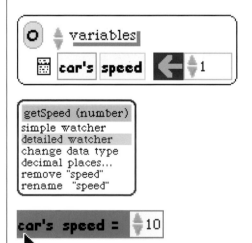

Hey! Can I
enter my mouse
in a race?

Continue by painting another car. Both cars should be drawn so that the direction they will go forward is up. This means that the heading of the cars will be set to zero. Name each car after its color.

Paint a straight line using the paint tools. This will be the starting line for the race. Place it at the bottom of the project. Paint another line and place it above the first one. This will be the finish line.

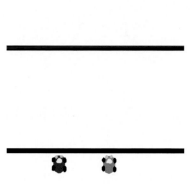

Navigator

Supplies

Bring up the tiles for each car and add a *new variable* to them. Name the variable "speed." Set the speed of each car to a random number. For this project, make the maximum value of the random number the same for both cars.

Come on — I want to win this race!!!

Create scripts for both cars that will tell the car to go forward by its variable speed, as shown earlier in this project.

From each of the cars' speed tiles, get a detailed watcher.

When the scripts are made, click on the **normal** button at the top of the scriptor and select "paused" from the menu.

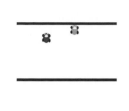

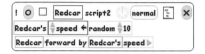

Drag out a set of **stop step go** buttons from the Supplies flap.

Click on the **step** button. Watch as the numbers in the detailed watchers change to represent the random number that is generated by the variable "speed." Click on the **go** button. Does the same car always reach the finish line first? If so, why? If not, why not?

How about having some races? I'll be the starter!

27

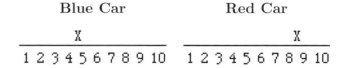

Using the concepts of *mean* and *mode* you can plot out the speed at which each car moves with each tick of the clock. In this way it is possible to find the average speed of each car.

Line plots can be used to determine the mean and the mode of each car's speed. The numbers plotted on the grid will be determined by the random number that is generated each time the step button is pressed.

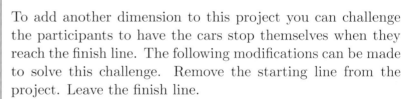

The test should be run at least ten times and the results shown on the line plot. Then the average speed should be determined as well as the mode of each of the cars.

At this point you can predict, based on your findings, which car you think would win if the two cars were to race. You would also want to explain why you come to this conclusion, and prove it with your data.

To add another dimension to this project you can challenge the participants to have the cars stop themselves when they reach the finish line. The following modifications can be made to solve this challenge. Remove the starting line from the project. Leave the finish line.

There are two cars in the project and each car has a script. It is good practice to name the scripts. This will also help as the projects become more challenging.

Click on the word "script" at the top of each scriptor to name it. In the following example the script is named "racing."

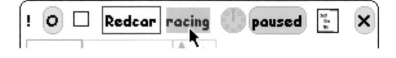

Add a "Test" tile to the script of each car.

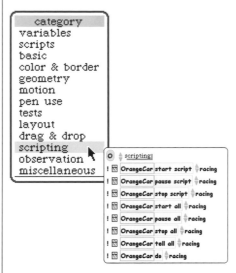

Add "color sees" tiles to each of the scripts. To find the tile that is needed to stop the cars as they cross the finish line, select the **scripting** category. Since the script has been named, all the tiles in this category will have the name of the script as part of their tiles. Select the "pause script" tiles and place them next to "Yes" in the test. Change the location of the "speed" and "forward by" tiles into the "No" position

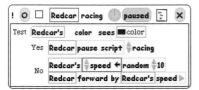

of the tests. (See the examples below.) Remember to start the race: click the **go** button which will start all scripts.

As each car crosses the finish line it will stop itself. In order to get the cars to stop each other once *one* of them has crossed the

finish line requires just one more set of tiles. These tiles are found in the **scripting** category of each of the cars. Choose the "pause script" tiles for each of the cars and place them below each of the other pause scripts in the "Yes" portion of the test.

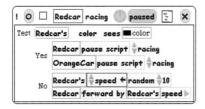

There are other ways to solve this problem. The method described above is just one of them.

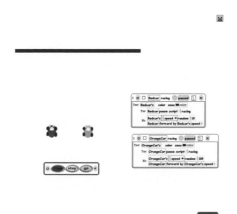

Challenges

- Line the cars up to race each other. How can you get the cars to stop themselves when they reach the finish line?

- How many other ways can you think of to make both cars stop when one of them crosses the finish line?

- Create a clock or timer that will keep time and show you how long it takes the winning car to cross the finish line.

- Create a starter for the race. (An object that starts all the cars at the same time.)

- How would you create a "reset button" that would return the cars to their original positions when the race is over?

Project 6

More Fun
with
Racing Cars

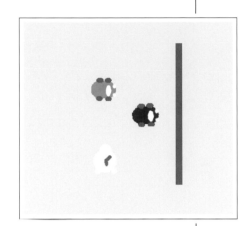

This project gives learners an opportunity to think more about the concepts which have been presented in previous projects.

The learners will have the chance to create a new variable (called time) and will continue to use and combine many of the Etoy tools such as buttons, reset scripts and conditional statements.

This project extends learning by setting up a new series of challenges based on two racing cars. It also reinforces understanding of the projects the learners have already completed.

I've got an idea that will solve the clock challenge and maybe they'll let me be the starter.

Project Prerequisites: Squeak

- Making buttons.

- Changing the label of a button.

- Changing the way in which a script will run.

Related Math Concepts

- The power of addition: "increase by."

The Timer

Here is one way to solve the "timer challenge." Draw a simple clock and name it. Create a variable in the clock called "time", then create a script that tells "time" to "increase by" 1.

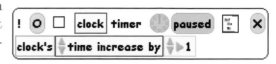

MouseDown on the clock within the script and change the "tick time" so that the clock ticks once per second.

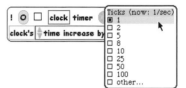

Get a detailed watcher for this script.

To use the timer to show how long it takes the winning car to cross the finish line requires only the addition of one set of tiles to both cars' scripts. In the "Yes" portion of the test, add

the tiles shown on the left to the script of each car.

Here is an example of one of those scripts:

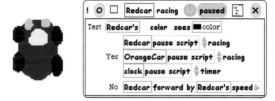

One way to solve the "starter challenge" is to use a button  from the Supplies flap. Bring up the handles of the button. Click on the red "menu" handle of the button.

Change the label of the button to "starter."

Create a script for this button that will start all of the other scripts. For example:

MouseDown on the **paused** button at the top of the script. Select "mouseUp" so that the script will run each time you release the mouse over the button.

Finally, make a button that will reset all of the scripts so that the race can run many times. You need to know the *x and y coordinates of each car* at the start of the race so that we can return them to this starting location. The **reset** button will return the cars to the start location and will reset the clock to zero.

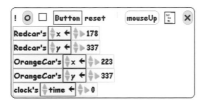

Notes

- There are many solutions to these challenges; those presented here are just one way in which the problems can be solved.

- It is good practice to create reset routines (scripts).

Project 7

The Great Race

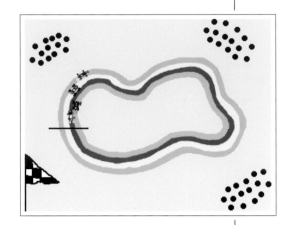

The Great Race is the culmination of all the preceding projects. It allows the learners to use the concepts they've acquired up to this point and for the first time take an individually-created and scripted object and bring it into a shared project.

Students can strategize how they might script their car to win a race on a muticolored, multiple-lane track. This encourages thinking about the total length of each lane and whether a car racing in one lane might have an advantage over another. Learners can be challenged to determine the length of each lane in order to set a fair starting point for each car in its lane.

This project also promotes group interaction and peer support as individual cars compete in each race.

I'm ready for
The Great Race!

Project Prerequisites: Squeak

- Drawing objects.
- Use of "test" tiles.
- Use of "color sees" tiles.
- Use of "random" tiles.
- Category in viewer: **scripting**.
- Naming scripts.

Related Math Concepts

- "Feedback" controlling the behavior of an object.
- Staggered starting points that equalize distances travelled on different lanes.

Curricular Objectives

- Synthesize the concepts learned earlier to create a car that will compete with others on a multi-lane track.

The Great Race

In this project several cars will race against each other on a multi-lane track.

For this activity, each of the participants are challenged to paint the most creative car they can imagine. The only requirement for the car is that it have headlights. The headlights will act as the car's sensors.

The participants are challenged to write a script for their car that uses the "color sees" tiles, a variable called "speed" and a random number. They will first need to practice on their own track to find how best to adjust the random speed and the steering controls of the car to maneuver as quickly as possible while remaining safely within their lane on the track.

The cars will then be "imported" into a single project that contains one large race track. The track will have four lanes, each lane a different color.

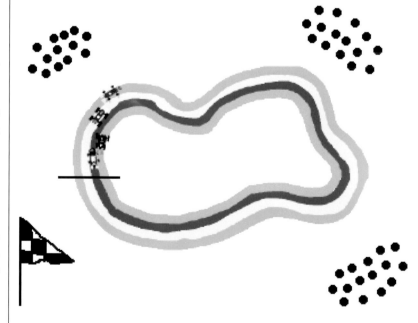

As each car is completed, its project can be opened on a networked computer and a copy of the car added to the Supplies flap of the shared "Great Race" project. Each of the race entrants can draw a number indicating the lane in which their car will race.

Some discussion should take place. Should all cars start at the same place? Does any particular lane have an advantage over the others? A decision should be made and the cars placed on the track and in their lane at an appropriate starting place.

The rules of the race need to be explained to all of the participants. As the lane assignments are given, each participant should be given time to modify their scripts so that their car will run correctly on the new track with the new colors. They should be given time to test the random speed of their car on the new track to see if they want to change its upper limit. No car may interfere with any other car during the race and must stay within its own lane throughout the race. Any interference of one car with another is an automatic disqualification. The first car to cross the finish line is declared the winner.

Notes

- Prepare yourself for an exciting session! The participants will enthusiastically cheer on their car and the cars of the other participants.

- To add a special feature to the race, winners from each heat can compete against each other to determine the fastest car in the entire group. Prizes can be awarded, too.

And the winner is...

Creating animations is one use of "increase by." The following is a simple way that objects can be transformed and brought to life using this powerful idea. It is also a time that you can break away from the "Drive-a-Car" curriculum and have fun creating a variety of animated objects.

Start a new project. Bring up the paint tools and use the largest circle (brush size) to paint a ball. Paint a highlight on the ball. Paint an ellipse a short distance beneath the ball; this will represent the ball's shadow.

Using this first painting as your guide, bring up the paint tools again. Paint a second shadow on top of the first one. Paint a second ball; this time paint the ball slightly lower than the original one.

Repeat this sequence until you have as many balls that you want in your sequence. These sequences are called *inbetweens*.

Make the last ball in the sequence flatter than the others. Exaggeration is often used in animation; the way that you paint your objects can reinforce the way they appear to move.

Here is an example of my 4 frames.

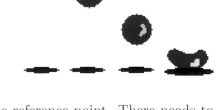

All of your ball paintings in the sequence must have the same reference point. There needs to be one thing in each of them that remains exactly the same and in the same place. As the ball is dropping the shadow beneath it should not move. In this example, the shadow is the reference point.

MouseOver your first painting and bring up its handles. Then MouseDown on the blue "rotation" handle. Turn it to the right or left.

 This symbol will appear in the center of your painting. It indicates the center of rotation of the object *and* the reference point for animation. Imagine a circle drawn around the painting. The ball and the shadow are both rotating around the center point of the circle.

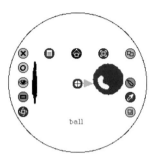

In order for our animation to run smoothly, the center of rotation must be set to the same location in each of our paintings. If we move the center of rotation symbol below the ball's shadow, we change its center of rotation.

In order to change the center of rotation, hold down the shift key while dragging the center of rotation symbol to its new position. In this example, the center of rotation was moved from the center to just below the ball's shadow in every painting of the ball.

Old center of rotation 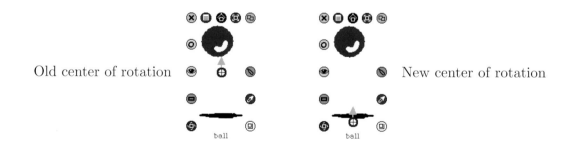 New center of rotation

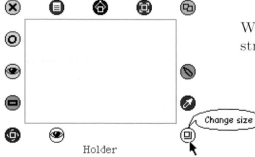

Get a Holder from the Supplies flap. Bring it on to the World. MouseDown on the yellow "change size" handle and stretch the holder to lengthen it.

Bring up the handles of your first ball painting. MouseDown on the green "duplicate" handle to make a copy of this painting. Drag it into the holder. Make sure that your **cursor is in the holder** before you MouseUp.

Drag each of the remaining *original* paintings into the holder. Once all of the paintings are in the holder, make a duplicate of each of them and place them as shown in the example. This sequence will make the ball bounce animation flow smoothly. The ball will bounce to its shadow and then bounce back up again.

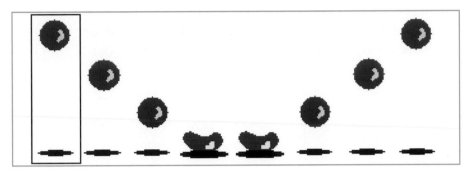

The **black rectangle** around the first ball represents the cursor.

Bring up the viewer for the ball. From the ball's **graphics** category, drag out the tiles "ball look like dot" and drop them into the World.

Bring up the viewer for the "Holder". From the category menu select "play-field". From the tiles that appear, select the tiles "Holder's playerAtCursor" and drop them over the word "dot" in your script.

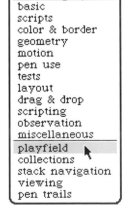

From the holder's basic category select the tiles "Holder's cursor". Drag these tiles out by the green assignment arrow.

Place these tiles in your script.

  ⟵

Click on the up arrow found to the right of the word "cursor."

| ! ⊙ ☐ | ball | script1 | normal | ▤ | ✖ |

ball look like Holder's playerAtCursor
Holder's ⇕cursor ← ⇕▶1

Continue clicking until you have changed the tile to read "increase by".

| ! ⊙ ☐ | ball | script1 | normal | ▤ | ✖ |

ball look like Holder's playerAtCursor
Holder's ⇕cursor increase by ⇕▶1

Click on the small clock at the top of your scriptor to start your animation.
Try reversing the order of the tiles in the script. What happens?

At this stage of the curriculum it is important to emphasize the role of off-computer activities to the participant's understanding of the ideas and concepts conveyed through the computer-based projects.

People are often sidetracked trying to find an exact answer to a problem. The important idea here is to get the learners to understand the larger concept rather than trying to find an exact answer. Science makes maps of the universe. As Einstein pointed out, the more mathematics refers to reality the less it is certain, and the more it is certain the less it refers to reality.

Part of this curriculum entails asking the participants to think about the distance between dots or trails left behind by their objects. The point is that they see an increase in distance from dot to dot; it is not important that they know by exactly how much that distance increases. This off-computer measuring activity can help participants understand how difficult accurate measurement can be, how our measurements may vary when using different measuring devices and that each answer may not necessarily be an exact answer — but rather an approximation. It is important to get the students to think about how much error is "allowable" and reasonable, and when it may be time to take another measurement entirely.

The following is an off-computer "excursion" that can help achieve a better understanding of this concept.

Materials:

- bicycle tires (all the same type and size);

- centimeter cubes;

- ribbon;

- yarn;

- click wheels;

- measuring tapes.

The participants can be divided into groups. Each group is given a different set of tools for measuring the circumference of a bicycle tire:

      Group 1   Centimeter cubes.
      Group 2   Ribbon and click wheel.
      Group 3   Yarn and measuring tape.

Everyone in the group is given the task of measuring the circumference of the tire using their assigned measuring device. After completing the task they should compare their results with the results of the other members of their group. They should also compare their results with the other groups that used different measuring devices to measure their tires.

Since all of the tires appear to be the same, a rich discussion should take place as to how it is possible for everyone to measure the same object and yet obtain a variety of answers. What are the variables that come into play when performing this measuring task? How much room is there for error? Is an exact measurement important? Can we make an approximation of the circumference based on all of the measurements that were taken?

Another discussion may evolve around whether the tires are in fact the exact same size. They may all be stamped with the same measurments, but are they really the same size? What is the margin of error (technically known as *tolerance*) that the manufacturer allows? Is it important for the tire to *be* exactly a certain size?

It is important for the participants to walk away with an understanding that the world is not exact and there cannot be an exact answer to many questions. An approximation can be a valid answer. There are many variables that have an effect on the outcome of an event. When creating simulations, we cannot recreate every variable that might have an affect on the outcome of an experiment. It is important to conclude that an approximation is a valid answer to draw from experimentation.

My tire is *this* big...

Project 8

Thinking About "Speed"

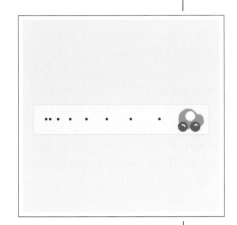

In this project learners will paint a car from a side view. The side view will help to visualize the car's speed.

This project provides another example which makes use of the powerful idea "increase by." The car will be scripted to move along its x axis (instead of moving "forward by"). In this example both the "car's x" will increase and the "car's speed" will increase by either a constant or a changing number.

Adding the use of a pen trail, drawn in a "dots style" in this project, learners can see patterns made by their car as it moves. They can be asked to think about the pattern of the dots and how it might differ when the car's speed is constant and when it increases, allowing for the further exploration of motion and acceleration.

Project Prerequisites: Squeak

- Making buttons.

- Changing the labels of buttons.

- Making scripts for buttons.

- Changing the way in which a script will run.

- Renaming playfields.

Related Math Concepts

- The difference between a number that is constant and one that is constantly increasing.

- The concept of cumulative.

- Movement along the x axis.

- Using "increase by" to create acceleration.

- Measurement.

- Using variables.

Curricular Objectives

- Use "increase by" to show acceleration.

- Use tools other than rulers as measuring devices.

- Use visual information to form a hypothesis.

For this project, a new car must be painted. This time the car should be painted from its side view, rather than the top view that we have used in the previous projects.

After the car has been painted, drag a playfield out of the Supplies flap and name it **home**. Place the car into this playfield.

Home

Drag another playfield out of the supplies flap and name it **TestArea**.

Bring up the tiles for the car. From the category **pen use**, change the following tiles:

- Change "pen down" to "true";
- Change "pen size" to "3";
- Change "trailStyle" to "dots."

For example:

The **home** playfield will act as a place to which the car will return after we have run each of our tests in the **TestArea**. Bring up the tiles for the playfield **home**. From the **collections** category select the tiles "home include" and place them in the world. Bring up the tiles for the **TestArea**. From the category **pen use**, select the tiles "TestArea" and "clear all pen trails" and drop them into the script.

Bring up the handles for the car. Click on the orange ● handle to get a tile that represents the car. Place it next to the "home" and "include" tiles in the script.

Each time the exclamation point of this script is clicked, the car will return to **home** and all the dots in the **TestArea** will be cleared. This is a valuable way to set the project back to its original state.

Bring up the scripting tiles for the car. Here are the following things that need to be created in the script:

- The car needs a variable called "speed".

- Speed should be set to a number.

- The car's "x" should increase by the "car's speed".

Instead of the car simply moving forward, it is now moving along its x axis by its speed.

Place the car in the **TestArea**. Drag the **stop step go** buttons from the Supplies flap. Click on the  button. Notice that the dots left behind as the car moves forward are the same distance apart.

The next step is to get the car to *accelerate* rather than maintaining a constant speed. To do this it is only necessary to change one tile in the car's script. Change the "car's speed" in the script to **increase by**. It is a good idea to begin with a small number, like 5.

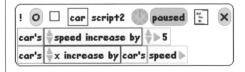

Let's go faster!!!

At this point we want to add a tile to the **home** script. Because "increase by" has been added to the "speed" variable, the value of "speed" will increase each time the script is activated. It is *cumulative*. The first time the script is activated the value of "speed" will become 5, but the next time it will become 10 and then 15 and 20, and so on. It is important to make sure that each time the simulation is started, the value of the variable "speed" is *set back to 0*.

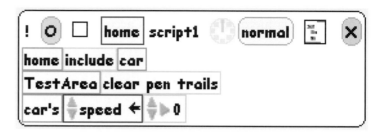

Here is another way of creating a button that will activate this script. Click on the word "home" at the top of the scriptor window. When the menu appears, select "button to fire this script". Once the button is created, dismiss the script by clicking on the tan circle.

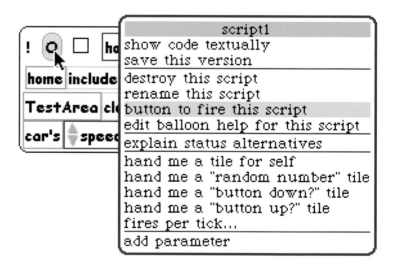

Home script1   Button to fire the script.

Place the car back in the **TestArea**.

Click on the  button and observe what happens. Discuss the difference between the line of dots laid down by the car this time and the line of dots laid down by the car the first time.

I can hardly keep up with this guy!

Speed is increasing (the car is accelerating).

Speed is constant (no acceleration).

It might help the discussion if a watcher is used to observe the variable "speed". It is important to relate what is happening to the value of speed and the effect it has on the car's "x" and then relate this to the fact that the dots left behind by the car are getting farther apart. Note that the "speed" of the car is increasing by 5 each time the script is fired, causing the car to increase the distance it travels along the x axis with each step. The car is going faster with each firing of the script. The car is *accelerating*.

The watcher reports the car's speed with each firing of the script.

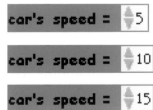

Note

- You might consider having the participants put their thoughts and observations right into the Squeak project. This can be done by dragging a **Book** out of the Supplies flap and dropping it onto the World. Then drag a **Text** from the Supplies flap and drop it onto the book.

Project 9

From Cars to Balls

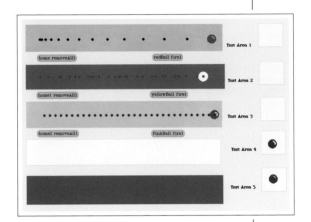

This project serves as a model to provoke transfer of learning as we transition from cars to the realm of falling balls and the exploration of gravity. It should reinforce each learner's understanding of the concepts of *constant*, *random* and *increasing* speed.

Most learners will easily make the transition in thinking about their object, previously as "car" now as "ball," seeing it as an abstract object wearing a "costume." Others may need reminding that this "ball" is nothing new and that creating the same scripts they made for their car will work just as well with this object called "ball."

Asking students to create scripts for the examples provided and then to write about each example can serve as a form of assessment for the teacher to determine the level of understanding of these concepts reached by each student.

Project Prerequisites: Squeak

- Creating and naming scripts.
- Creating variables.
- Using random tiles.
- Making buttons.
- Creating reset scripts.
- Creating animation.
- Using and renaming playfields.
- Creating dot trails.

Related Math Concepts

- Understanding the difference between numbers that are:
    - constants;
    - increasing by a fixed amount;
    - changing randomly.

Curricular Objectives

- Give the participants the opportunity to use and articulate what they have learned in order to identify, solve and recreate the problems presented in this small quiz.

This project can be prepared in advance to challenge students to demonstrate what they've learned and understood about the concepts presented in the previous projects. Once prepared, the project can be downloaded to each student's local computer.

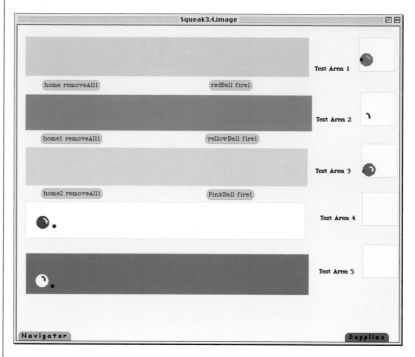

Begin by creating ten playfields. The five fields on the left, as shown in the example above, act as "test areas" for the action to take place. The five fields on the right act as "home fields" to which the ball returns after being removed from the test area by means of a "reset" script.

redBall fire1   home removeAll1

The buttons above are examples of the buttons that were created and placed below each of the test areas. The **fire** buttons will cause a particular action to take place in the test area above it. Each time the button is clicked, the ball will move along its x axis according to the rules created in the script. The **removeAll** buttons will remove the ball and all dots from the field and place the original ball back in its home field.

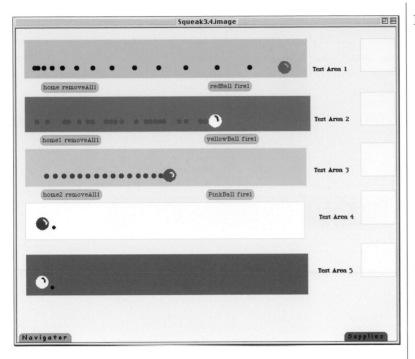

RemoveAll button and script:

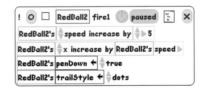

BallFire button and scripts:

Acceleration

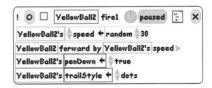

The balls move along the x axis. The first ball moves along the x axis and *accelerates*, the second moves *randomly* and the last one moves by a *constant* amount. The dots left behind are a visual clue to help determine what is happening in each simulation.

The participants can be asked to look at each example and to recreate any two of the three actions that take place in the playfields. They need to create the buttons that will fire each of their scripts and the buttons that will reset them. They create their own simulations in the two playfields at the bottom of the project. As the final step, the participants can drag a **Book** from the Supplies flap and use it to articulate their solutions to the problems. (Don't forget to drop a **Text** into the book too.) They can then share their solutions with other participants.

Random

Book

Constant

Children love participating in all aspects of this excursion.

Materials Needed:
- A shotput.
- An apple.
- A sponge ball.
- A croquet ball.
- A drilled out shotput.
- Stop watches.
- A video camera.
- A way of digitizing the video footage and storing it on a computer.
- An outdoor area with a roof at least 8 feet high from which the balls can be dropped.

Before starting this excursion, which will be videotaped, all of the balls and the apple should be passed around the group so that everyone can touch them and get a sense of the weight of each object. A typical shotput ball might weigh 12 lbs. Its weight surprises participants and they might find it difficult to hold in one hand.

Once all participants have had the chance to hold each of the objects, predictions can be made about which object (if any), when dropped from a roof, will fall to the ground the fastest. For example, in our classroom the participants ranked each object from one to five. If they felt that any two of the objects might hit the ground at the same time, they gave them the same ranking.

They wrote up their predictions and explained the rationale behind their thinking.

Now go outside and drop each of the objects off the roof, while videotaping the event. The participants should have stop watches so that they can record how long it takes each object to hit the ground.

Later the objects can be dropped in pairs to test hypotheses as to which might fall to the ground the fastest. The importance of using stop watches is for the participants to realize that it takes approximately the same amount of time for each object to hit the ground regardless of its weight.

After all the objects have been dropped and videotaped (it is wise to do this several times) you can use the footage in a number of ways. You might choose to have the participants watch the footage immediately after the outdoor activity. This can generate a rich discussion about what they believed they saw and what actually happened. Careful observation of the video will demonstrate how a variety of variables may have affected the outcome of each drop.

This excursion also takes advantage of Squeak's multimedia capabilities. Squeak allows you to bring video frames into a project and then animate these frames to create movies (or manipulate the images in other ways). This is a critical part of the ball-dropping experiment and obviously this method can be used in a variety of contexts.

You'll need to bring the video into the computer as a set of still "jpeg" images. Both *iMovie* and *Windows Movie Maker* can save a video sequence as a series of jpeg images.

Since it will only take each ball about a second to hit the ground, the movie will be about 30 frames of jpeg images in length. To bring the jpegs into Squeak, go to the Navigator flap and MouseDown for a few seconds on the **Find** button. Select "find any file" from the options. Load the jpeg images into your Squeak project. Bringing every sixth frame (or jpeg image) into your project will result in something that looks like this:

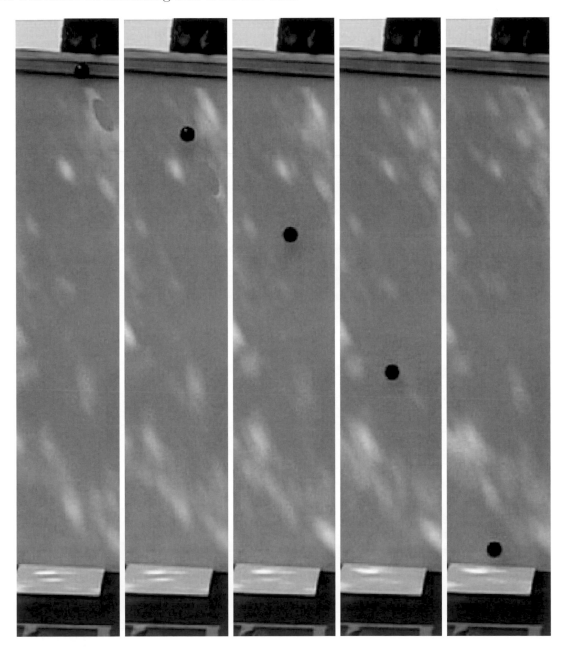

That's all for this excursion, but the learners will be using these frames in the next several projects as they continue to explore gravity and acceleration.

Project 10

Another Look at Falling Balls

This Etoy project follows on from the excursions described previously. Ideally, learners should have already engaged in a variety of measurement activities to understand how difficult it is to find an "exact" number or answer to any given problem, and to practice the art of estimation and approximation.

Students also should have had the concrete experience of watching a variety of objects dropped from a roof after having theorized what would happen. Sometimes what we insist we have "seen with our own eyes" is merely what we believe we saw, based upon misconception rather than what really happened.

This project allows students to take another look at what happened when the balls were dropped and provides a way to enable both the deconstruction and reconstruction of the event. The project also provides a way to "stop time." What we can see when time is stopped might look quite different from what we thought we saw in a fleeting moment of "real time."

Bringing individual video frames into the project allows students to manipulate a visualization of the event. Providing a view not possible in the real world offers learners additional opportunities to understand the phenomenon.

Project Prerequisites: Squeak

- Using repainting tools.

Related Math Concepts

- Movement along the y axis.

Curricular Objectives

- Give the participants the opportunity to use what they have learned about acceleration in the drive-a-car project and apply it to what they are seeing in the gravity project.

I'm falling!

Begin this project by loading the video frames into a new project, or reloading your previously-saved project.

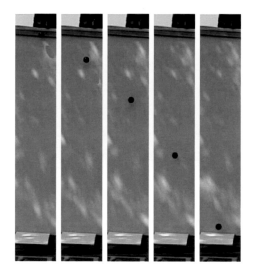

Upon seeing these frames, some learners will get an immediate "aha!" and see a pattern. Others may have a harder time with this representation. To recreate what was seen when the experiment was performed outside, and to get the ball to appear to fall in a straight line, the jpeg frames can be cut and stacked.

Bring up the handles of the second frame. Select the "repaint" handle. Leaving the ball in the frame, erase everything above it. Do that for each of the remaining frames.

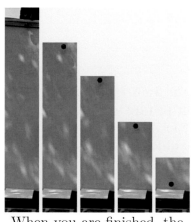

When you are finished, the frames should look like this.

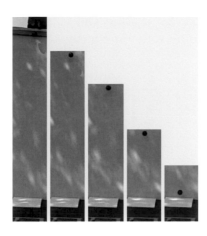

Once the frames have all been "trimmed," the next step is to stack them neatly one on top of the other.

Note:

At this time the participants in our class were eager to share what they thought they were seeing. Many students immediately saw that the ball appeared to be accelerating as it fell to the ground.

The distance between the balls appeared to be increasing. Some students even returned to their car project and rotated it so that they could compare the two. A transfer of learning had occured.

Starting with the second frame, move it on top of the first frame. Use the bottom of each frame as a guide for placing the frames on top of each other.

When all the frames are stacked on top of each other, your picture will look like this. At this stage, participants can see that the speed of the falling object is increasing.

Project 11

"Measuring" the Distance

This project allows for the continued manipulation and examination of the "cut and stacked" video frames. It is intended to help students gain a deeper understanding of the meaning of the pattern made by the falling ball.

For some students, seeing the pattern discovered in Project 10 is not enough to "prove" that the ball was accelerating as it fell. Using transparent "sticky notes" as measuring devices to investigate the distance between successive "snapshots" of the ball provides another visualization of its behavior.

After using the "sticky notes" to measure, students can stack them to make a graph — creating yet another visualization to see that each ball's speed was indeed constantly increasing as it fell to the ground.

Project Prerequisites: Squeak

- Using rectangles as measuring devices.

- Using simple and detailed watchers.

Related Math Concepts

- Movement along the y axis.

- Understanding the power of "increase by" using negative numbers.

Science Concept

- Looking at how acceleration becomes a key factor to understanding the force of gravity on a falling object.

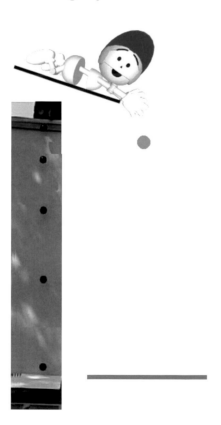

The stacked video frames created in Project 10 are the starting point for this project. Now that the falling ball is aligned in a straight column, rectangular sticky notes torn off the Sticky Pad (found in the Supplies flap) can be used to measure the distance between each ball. Each rectangle will be a different color.

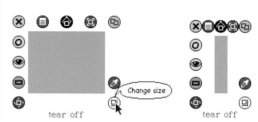

The measurement should be done from the bottom of the first ball to the bottom of the next ball, or as closely to that as possible. Some participants may chose to use a magnifier (from the Object Catalog in the Supplies flap) for accuracy.

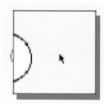

It is important for the learners to understand what is happening to the distance between each ball. Our students found a variety of ways to articulate what they thought they were seeing.

Before proceeding, the students may need to be reminded of the earlier measuring activity where they learned the importance of approximation.

Some students aligned their rectangles to form various bar graphs to visualize the acceleration. Some of them chose to use watchers to get a numeric value for the height or length of each rectangle. The increasing number confirmed the rate of change in the ball's speed.

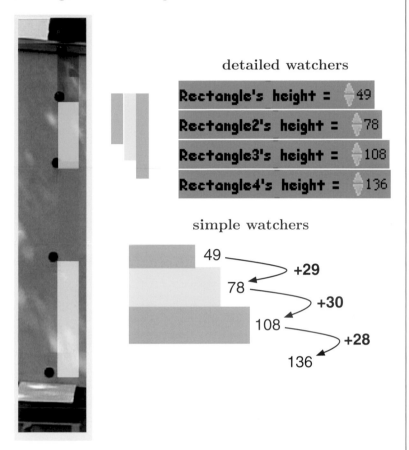

detailed watchers

Rectangle's height = 49

Rectangle2's height = 78

Rectangle3's height = 108

Rectangle4's height = 136

simple watchers

49
+29
78
+30
108
+28
136

Recalling the previous measurement excursion (and reminding the students what they learned about approximation and tolerance) may help them to see that the length of each bar (measured in pixels) is not only increasing but appears to be increasing at very close to a constant rate — in other words, a constant acceleration.

Some students chose to do the arithmetic that would tell them if the ball was accelerating as it fell and, if so, by how much. They subtracted the height of one rectangle from the height of the next to determine an approximate acceleration. At that point they could see the ball was indeed accelerating at a constant rate.

Finding the Magnifier

Drag the Object Catalog out of the Supplies flap.

Object Catalog

Select **alphabetic** from the catalog.

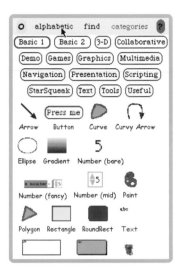

Select the letter **m**.

Select the **Magnifier** and drag it into the project.

Magnifier

This tool will magnify anything it passes over.

In this excursion, an animation will be created from the jpegs of the ball drop sequence.

Reload the jpeg sequence into a new Squeak project. Name the first frame of the sequence **dropMovie**. Next drag a **Holder** out of the Supplies flap and resize it to fit all of the frames of the ball drop sequence.

Drag a copy of the first frame into the holder. Next drag all of the remaining frames directly into the holder.

We're making a movie!!

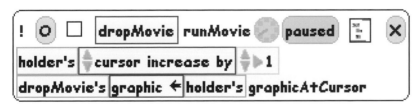

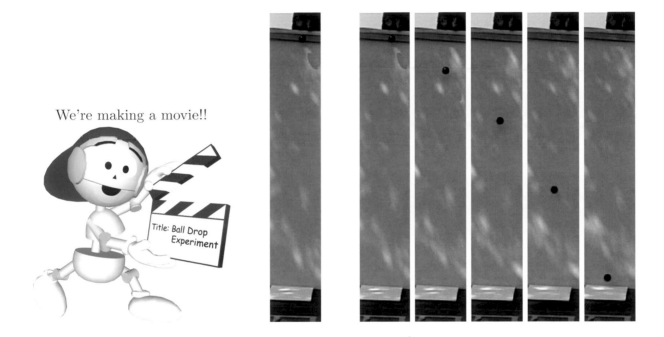

Bring up the scripting tiles for the frame called **dropMovie**. Create a script. Name the script **runMovie**.

This script will create an animated movie of the ball falling off the roof.

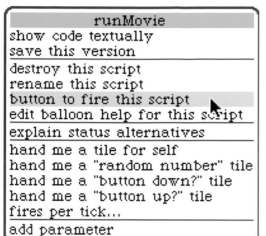

Once you have created the script, make a button that will fire the script. Rename the button **step-Movie**.

stepMovie

If you start the script it will run continuously, but if you click on the button the script will only fire once. With each additional click of the button, the script will step through the sequence of frames and animate the ball dropping.

Once the button is made, be sure to save this project. We'll need it again later.

We are ready to move on to the final project: a simulation of gravity using a painted ball. The ultimate challenge will be to make a painted ball "fall" at the same rate of acceleration as the ball in the movie. We want the painted ball and the ball in the movie to reach the bottom at the same time.

Boy, this is going to take some real thought. This *is* a good challenge!

Project 12

A Simulated Ball Drop

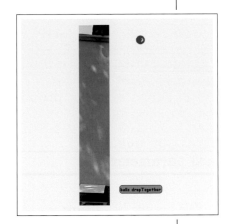

This is the culminating project in this series exploring acceleration and gravity. In this project learners will be challenged to paint a simulated ball and script it so that it models the acceleration of real-world objects caused by gravity.

The animated movie of the ball drop will then be brought into the project so that students can compare the drop of their ball with that of the ball in the video.

Creating this simulation requires learners to think about many of the concepts they've used in the previous projects — the creation of variables, the use of "increase by" and what it means to "increase by" a negative number.

Perhaps most importantly, it encourages students to think about creating and testing theories, to perform many tests to assess their hypotheses against these theories and to make models that simulate real-world phenomena.

Project Prerequisites: Squeak

- Creating and naming scripts.

- Creating variables.

- Creating reset scripts.

- Creating animations.

- Creating buttons.

- Creating and using watchers.

Related Math Concepts

- Understanding variables.

- Understanding the power of "increase by" using negative numbers.

- Movement along the y axis.

- Understanding the concept of acceleration.

Related Science Concepts

- Forming a hypothesis.

- Looking at how acceleration becomes a key factor to understanding the force of gravity on a falling object.

- Simulating the force of gravity on a falling object, using a model as a guide.

Begin a new Squeak project. Paint a ball and name it.

Bring up the scripting tiles for the ball. Create a variable and name it "speed".

Create a script in the ball called **drop**. This script will increase the "ball's speed" by a negative number, one yet to be determined. The example below will test what happens when the speed is increased by −10. The second line of the **drop** script will increase the "ball's y" by its speed.

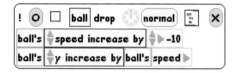

At this point you have a model of a constantly accelerating falling ball!

Next create a script to reset the "ball's speed" and the "ball's y" to their initial values. Name the script **reset**. Create a button that will fire this script. Get a detailed watcher for the variable "speed". The **reset** script will make it easier to set the ball and its speed back to their original values and locations.

Experiment and play with the number by which the speed is increasing. What happens? What happens if the ball's "y" does not increase by its speed?

Next open the project in which you saved the "ball drop" movie. Paint a new ball and place it alongside the ball in the **dropMovie** frame.

Run the animation continuously by setting the script to "ticking." Clicking on the **stepMovie** button will step through the animation.

The final challenge is to script the painted ball to drop at the same rate as the ball in the animation. Using what you've previously learned recreate the scripts for the painted ball to fall and to reset. *Note: When creating a **reset** button remember that since the movie begins with the ball in motion, its starting speed cannot be zero.*

Next create a script *in the **dropMovie** frames* that will reset the animation back to the first frame. Name the script **reset**. Create a button that will fire this script.

Finally create a script *in the ball* that makes the ball drop and the movie run at the same time. Name this script **dropTogether**. When you create a button that will fire this script, change the name of the button to **balls drop together**.

When the **dropTogether** script is run, there will be a need to test and retest and change the value of speed until the ball falls at the same rate as the ball in the animation.

In our classroom, when the learners succeeded, we heard the cries of success throughout the room. Not only had they successfully completed the challenge, but they had a far better understanding of the concept of gravity than they would have gained from reading a book.

Challenge

- In this book we've used Squeak to create both *animations* and *simulations*. Think about the differences between them. Why aren't they the same thing?

Some Final Notes

The projects in this book are just the beginning of what can be created with this powerful tool.

Our solutions are only suggestions, since there may be many ways to solve these interesting problems.

Squeak, as a tool for the teaching of math and science, has unlimited possiblilites!

See you in **Squeakland!!**

Our Human Condition "From Space"

Alan Kay

My favorite examples of early science, and a wonderful general metaphor for what science does, are the attempts at highly accurate map-making started by the Greeks, then lost for a thousand years, and then taken up again starting in the 15th century. By the end of the 1700s, people delighted in being able to buy a pocket globe of "The World As Seen From Space". 200 years later, we went out into space, looked back at the world, took pictures of it, and saw just what the 18th century map makers had already found out.

All scientific processes and knowledge have this character: they are attempts to "see" and represent things very accurately from vantage points that are not part of our normal commonsense guesses about the world — to "make the invisible somewhat visible". For most of human history our theories about ourselves and the world we lived on were mainly in terms of unsubstantiated beliefs rendered as comforting stories. A few hundred years ago we learned a new kind of seeing that allowed us to perceive the physical world as if "from space" with far fewer prejudices in the way. In the 21st century we need to not only do this for the physical world, but also to understand our whole human condition as if "from space", without the comforting stories, but with deeper understanding of how to deal with our natures and nurtures.

Maps, as with all of our representations for ideas, are quite arbitrary and don't automatically have any intrinsic claims to accuracy. For example, here are 3 maps. The first is a map from the Middle Ages, the second is a map from Tolkein's "Lord of the Rings", and the third is a map of the Mojave Desert. The medieval "T–O" map shows the world as they thought "it had to be", and includes the Garden of Eden (to the Far East at the top). The Mediterranean (the middle of the world) is the vertical of the "T", Jerusalem is at the center of the world at the joining of the "T", and the boot of Italy is just a bulge. The Tolkein map was made up in careful detail to help readers (and probably the author) to visualize the fictitious world of the Hobbit and Lord of the Rings. The map of the Mojave Desert was made last year using both advanced surveying methods and satellite imagery to guide the placement of features.

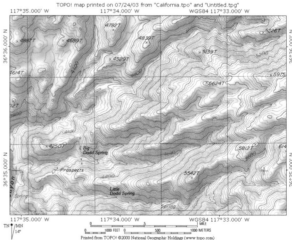

It is important to realize that from the standpoint of traditional logic, none of these maps is "true", in that none of them are in exact one-to-one correspondence with all the details of what they are trying to map. In other words each of these maps is a kind of story that is written mostly in images rather than words. Within a map we can do perfect logic — so for example, if Rome is north of Alexandria, and Paris is north of Rome then Paris is north of Alexandria. This internal logic works perfectly for all three maps. Mathematics is also a kind of mapping system that is set up to be completely consistent within itself — in fact, it includes the making of maps like these ("Earth Measuring" in Greek is "Geometry"). It's when we try to relate the maps to what they are supposed to represent "outside" that we run into difficulty and find that none of them are "true" in the sense of the truth that can obtain inside a map. But if you were dropped into the Mojave Desert, which "not-true" map would you choose to take with you? Many useful flavors of "false" really makes a difference in modern thinking!

From our standpoint, the reason to teach "the new thinking" that has flowered in the last 400 years is not to provide more technical jobs, or to "keep our country strong", or even to make better citizens. These are all good results that are byproducts of the new thinking, but the real reasons have to do with sanity and civilization. If the maps in our heads are unlike "what's out there" then we are at best what Alfred Korzybski termed "unsane". Our definition for actual insanity is simply when the maps in our heads, for whatever reasons, become so unlike "what's out there" (including what's in other people's maps) that it is noticeable and sometimes dangerous. Since we can't get maps to be exactly true, we are always somewhat unsane with respect to the physical world. Since our actual internal maps are not directly sharable, we are even more unsane in relation to each other's mappings of the world (including us). Because we think in terms of our internal maps — a kind of theatrical presentation of our beliefs back to ourselves — it is not too far a stretch to say that we live not in reality, but in a waking delusional hallucinatory dream that we like to call "reality". We definitely want to construct the "least false" version of this that we can!

Civilization is not a state of being that can be reached, nor the journey, but it is a manner of traveling. To me the most interesting and remarkable — even amazing — thing about science is that it is done by us even though we are creatures who only have stories of various kinds inside our heads and are much more set up to be interested in charging sabretoothed tigers than in centuries long climate changes. But the process of scientific thinking is able to deal with many of our own inabilities to think and other flaws in a strong enough manner to still come up with ever more accurate mappings of more and more complex parts of our universe. This is why we need to help all children in the world learn how to do it.

But why then are science and its mapping language — mathematics — deemed to be hard to learn? I believe that it is not because they are so intrinsically complicated, but rather they are amazingly simple yet very very different from normal human commonsense ways of thinking about things. It is gaining this quite unusual point of view about "what's out there?" and what it means to find and claim knowledge about it that is the main process of learning science. One way to look at this is that part of what has to be learned is a new kind of commonsense — Alan Cromer calls it "uncommonsense".

And, just as it doesn't require more than a normal mind to learn these ideas, it also doesn't require any major outlay of funds, though many people like to give the excuse that "science teaching isn't happening because we don't have computers, scientific equipment, books, etc.". Science is about 400 years old now, and we've had commercial personal computers for a little more than 20 years, so there were about 380 years in which science and math were learned without high tech. Some of the most important discoveries were done before the industrial revolution with very little equipment.

I think what is mainly lacking are adults who understand science who want to work with children and teachers regardless of the funding. Shame on my own profession! Most of us stay in the labs and away from children, parents, teachers and schools.

How can we learn science with "no money"? First and foremost, we have to learn how to observe and be interested in phenomena in a noncategorical way, i.e. we don't want to dismiss things after we've merely learned their names — there's a sense in which most things become almost invisible after we can recognize them and recall their names. So we have to find ways "to make the invisible

visible", to avoid "premature recognition". Science is all around us and much can be revealed just by being more careful about what we think we are seeing.

One of the ways to do this is by learning how to draw. As Betty Edwards (of "Drawing on the Right Side of the Brain" fame) points out, learning to draw is mostly learning to see (as opposed to learning to recognize). For many things we need to find ways to postpone quick recognition in favor of slower noticing. Typical "before and after" self-portraits by Edwards' students show a remarkable improvement.

This is somewhat different than the "art part" of the visual arts in that we are trying to mostly express the visual details of "what's there" rather than what we feel about it, but they are not at all exclusive. As my grandfather once remarked in an article he wrote for the Saturday Evening Post in 1904 about whether photography could be art: "Art enters in when we labor thoughtfully with some goal in mind; that is, when we cut loose from actions that are merely mechanical". Our feelings will appear in any of our carefully made creations.

Another good example of "high-noticing low-cost" is the measuring of the circumference of the bicycle tire excursion on page 43. Much of the philosophical gold in science is to be found in this noticing activity.

The students used different materials and got different answers, but were quite sure that there was an exact answer in centimeters (partly because schooling encourages them to get exact rather than real answers). One of the teachers also thought this because on the side of the tire it said it was 20 inches in diameter. The teacher "knew" that the circumference was $\pi \times$ diameter, that "π is 3.14", and "inches times 2.54 converts to 'centimeters'", etc., and multiplied it out to get the "exact circumference" of the tire = 159.512 cm. I suggested that they measure the diameter and they found it was actually more like 19 and 3/4 inches (it was uninflated)! This was a shock, since they were all set up to believe pretty much anything that was written down, and the idea of doing an independent test on something written down had not occurred to them.

That led to questions of inflating to different pressures, etc. But still most thought that there was an exact circumference. Then one of us contacted the tire manufacturer (who happened to be Korean) and there were many interesting and entertaining exchanges of email until an engineer was found who wrote back that "We don't actually know the circumference or diameter of the tire. We extrude them and cut them to a length that is 159.6 cm ± 1 millimeter tolerance!

This really shocked and impressed the children — the maker of the tire doesn't even know its diameter or circumference! — and it got them thinking much more powerful thoughts. Maybe you can't measure things exactly. Aren't there "atoms" down there? Don't they jiggle? Aren't atoms made of stuff that jiggles? And so forth. The analogy to "how long is a shoreline?" is a good one. The answer is partly due to the scale and tolerance of measurement. As Mandelbrot and others interested in fractals have shown, the length of a mathematical shoreline can be infinite, and physics shows us that the physical measurement could be "almost" as long (that is very long).

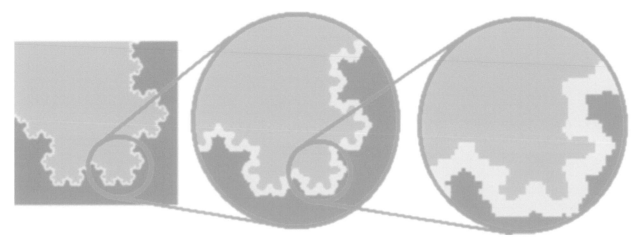

There are many ways to make use of the powerful idea of "tolerance". For example, when the children do their gravity project and come up with a model for what gravity does to objects near the surface of the earth, it is very important for them to realize that they can only measure to within one pixel on their computer screens and that they can also make little slips. A totally literal take on the measurements can cause them to miss seeing that uniform acceleration is what's going on. So they need to be tolerant of very small errors. On the other hand, they need to be quite vigilant about discrepancies that are outside of typical measuring errors. Historically, it was important for Galileo not to be able to measure really accurately how the balls rolled down the inclined plane, and for Newton not to know what the planet Mercury's orbit actually does when looked at closely.

Next year (2004) is the 400th anniversary of the first time in history that a good model was made of what happens when a body falls near the surface of the earth under the influence of gravity. Galileo didn't have home video cameras and computers and Squeak to come up with the model. He did his discovery "with no money" by being very diligent about observation and noticing until he found a way to pin down what was happening crisply enough to map it with mathematics.

How did he do it? There doesn't seem to be an absolutely definitive answer to this, but there are many stories about it which have been pieced together from Galileo's notes and writings. Galileo's father was a professional musician and Galileo had an excellent reputation as a musical amateur on a number of instruments including the flute and the lute.

He had been doing many experiments with inclined planes using uniformly sized balls made from different materials and having different weights. He discovered that same sized balls of different weights appeared to go down the inclined plane at the same rate of increase of speed regardless of angle.

One day he may have for fun idly rolled a ball or two down the neck of his lute. You can see that the frets of lutes and guitars are not evenly spaced. At some point he noticed that the clicks of the ball on the frets were almost regular and realized that the wider spacing of the frets was compensating for the increase in speed of the ball. Now a wonderful thing about lutes is that, unlike guitars, their frets are made of the same gut that is used from the strings and are simply tied on. So Galileo could move them. He started to move them until he could hear an absolutely regular sequence of clicks (at some point he probably started to tie the fret material across his inclined plane). When he got perfectly regular clicks, he measured the distances and found that the increase of speed (the acceleration) was constant!

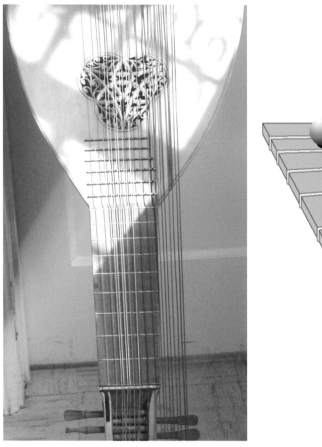
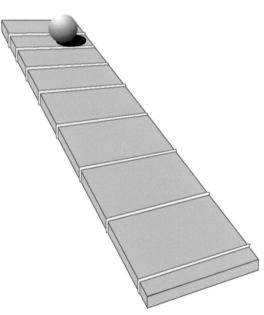

One of the important conclusions here is that there are many interesting real science probes that can be done with materials at hand if the teacher understands the real science. This is one way to do this investigation "with no money", and rolling a toy truck down the inclined plane carrying a baggie of ink with a pinhole, is another.

Don't let the lack of a computer or equipment slow you down. Science and math are all around us. The world we live in is a vast lab full of equipment, if it can be noticed. There are free public libraries even in the most disadvantaged parts of the US that contain books about how to do all of this: the knowledge doesn't cost money, but it does cost time and interest and focus.

You are reading this book because you are interested in all these issues — perhaps you found it in a free public library — whether or not you can afford a computer today. If you can't, there is still much you can do, just as there is so much real music that can be done with children without formal instruments. If you can afford the instrument — musical or computer — then you've just gotten wonderful amplifiers for your musical and mathematical and scientific impulses.

The computer quite naturally turns the math back into phenomena, thus providing a more complete full circle of "putting together" added to the "taking apart" nature of science. This is one of the most important uses of computers in adult science and engineering and thus the children and adults are strongly joined in the same art and sport, just as children's music is real music, and children's baseball and tennis are real versions of the sports.

A further insight is that the range and depth of constructions that the children can carry through are vastly extended by using a suitable computer environment. Many researchers have found that children are capable of deeper thoughts than they can easily build: for example, they can think very deeply about how robots and animals can make their way in the world and create truly subtle and profound programs on the computer that bring ideas to life in a way that is far beyond their abilities to construct physical versions of the ideas at their age.

In a few years the computers themselves will be almost free and will be part of a truly global communications network. So all the ideas described in this book are almost within reach of every child on the planet. But we still have to find ways to remember what is really important here.

The most critical distinction we have to keep in mind is that between "doing real science" and "learning about what scientists have done". This is similar to the distinction between "Music" and "Music Appreciation". The latter are worthwhile in both cases, but both quite need the learning of the real process in order to understand what the "Appreciation Knowledge" really means. For example, there are no important differences between being given a "holy book" full of assertions and being asked to memorize and believe them, and being given a "science book" full of assertions and being asked to memorize and believe them. As with the difference between two values of logic (true and false) and the many valued logic of science (lots of worthwhile falses) the difference between what science means when it says "we know that . . ." and what previous knowledge systems mean by this could hardly be larger. When science makes a claim about "knowing", it is so different from previous uses that it should not have tried to reuse "know" as the word for this, because what is meant is: "We have an excellent map-model for this that works thus and so with this amount of tolerance and doesn't map as well as we'd like here and there, and by the way, here's how you can help check this out and make your own criticisms, etc."

I hope that the projects presented in this book and what you've read so far will convince you that these activities are not only "math and science", but deep, real, and important aspects of mathematics and science. What if more issues than those of the physical world were thought about in this slower, suspended-perception, skeptical, careful, powerful, and map-and-model building manner? If you think that things would be vastly different and improved for the benefit of all humans, than please help children learn to think much better than most adults do today.

Can you speak "Squeak?"

Assignment Arrow
The green arrow on purple background found in an object's viewer. Using this arrow in a script will assign a value to a specific property of that object.

Etoy
A Squeak-based, "electronic" or "educational" project which might be a simulation, model, story or game created by a child or adult. An Etoy might help illustrate or give insight into a concept or powerful idea.

Flap
Navigational commands, supplies, and scripting tiles are all contained in flaps. Flaps are partially transparent and can be used to "store" additional items the user might like to keep handy for frequent use. The Squeak plug-in comes with two visible flaps as the default: Navigator and Supplies.

Star

Halo
When any object is selected (Alt-click or Command-click) a "halo" of "handles" will appear.

Handles
The colored icons surrounding an object. Each of these allow for different manipulation of and change to that object. See the "Handles Tutorial" on www.squeakland.org/etoys/tutorials to learn what each handle does. Each handle is also supplied with balloon help to inform you of its function.

Navigator
The orange flap found at the bottom-left of the World. When opened it contains options for navigating, collaborating, publishing (saving), painting and creating new projects.

Object
The unit of creation in Squeak. Everything is an object in Squeak! By sending messages (commands or scripts) to objects we can communicate with them and invoke behaviors.

Object Catalog

The Object Catalog is found in the Supplies flap. It is a searchable tool that lets you browse a variety of Squeak objects. It contains several categories as well as an alphabetic listing of all objects.

Pane

A section or category in an object's viewer. One can choose to have between one and four viewable "panes" in an object's viewer by clicking on the "mini-viewer" on the top left. Panes in the viewer are eliminated by clicking on its **remove** button.

Pens

As in Logo, any object can leave pen trails as it moves. Pens can be found in their own category **Pen Use** in an object's viewer. Setting "pen down" to "true" will leave a marked trail on the World. Note: Pen trails can only be left on the "World" or on a playfield, not on a painted background.

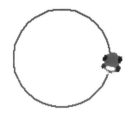

Playfield

A playfield is a type of object that can be found in the Supplies flap. Playfields can be the basis of a "sub project" or illustration within another project. Many playfields can be placed on a "World" and become part of a project.

Playfield

Plug-In

A plug-in is a piece of software that is used to expand the functionality of an existing program during its runtime. Once the Squeak plug-in is installed on your computer, Squeak projects become fully interactive. Plug-ins do not need to be loaded or unloaded when used, they will execute themselves when called upon to do so by the parent program or project. There are many plug-ins that provide both form and functionality (for example: QuickTime, Shockwave and Flash players, and so on).

Project

A project is the "hyper-document" in Squeak. Projects are created, published (saved), shared and exchanged. In word processing, we create documents; in Squeak we create projects.

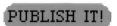

Publishing

Saving in Squeak is known as publishing. A project can be published to your computer's hard drive, or to a server so that it can be shared. Holding down the **Publish It!** button on the gold Navigator flap will show several publishing options.

Script/Scriptor

Objects can be sent messages and instructions by combining tiles and running them inside a "Scriptor." Before a script is created for an object, the "Scripts" category in the viewer only contains an "empty script." It is good practice to name your scripts as you create them. Scripts can be dismissed or hidden by clicking on the tan circle to the right of the exclamation point.

Sketch

Sketch

Any painted object, before it is named, is a sketch. It is good practice to name your sketches after painting and keeping them.

Sticky Pad

Sticky Pad

A sticky pad is a note pad filled with translucent "notes" of various pastel colors. Sticky notes can be "torn off" the pad and used for project annotation or a variety of purposes. Some of the projects in this book suggest using sticky notes as measuring devices.

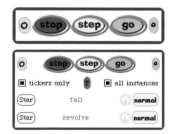

Stop-Step-Go Buttons (All Scripts tool)

The set of **stop step go** buttons found in the Supplies flap will run (and stop) all scripts in a project. Clicking the small blue button next to the **go** button will expand the buttons into the **All Scripts** tool. This tool shows *all* scripts in a project and can be very useful when reviewing other peoples' projects to understand how they were constructed.

Tab

Tabs are used to open and close flaps such as viewers, Supplies and the Navigator. Tabs are created for objects once a sketch has been "kept" and its viewer selected by clicking on the turquoise "eyeball" handle. A small thumbnail drawing of the sketch is shown on its tab. The tab can be dismissed (but not lost) by clicking the small tan circle at the top of the object's viewer, just to the right of the tab. If the tab has been dismissed, it can be recalled by selecting the object (revealing its handles) and selecting the turquoise "eyeball" handle.

Tiles

Tiles are the units used for constructing messages and scripts to send instructions to objects. Tiles are primarily found in an object's viewer. Tiles connected together form a "string."

Viewer

An object's viewer is revealed when clicking on the turquoise "eyeball" handle of any object. The viewer shows categories of properties and instructions for the object, represented by tiles. Clicking the yellow exclamation point in the viewer will run that particular instruction once (holding the exclamation point will repeat the action). Values of properties such as "x", "y" and "heading" are also shown in the object's viewer. There are several categories in the viewer. Clicking on the green arrowheads next to any category (for example, "basic") will toggle between the categories. Adding panes to the viewer (by clicking on the "miniviewer" icon in the viewer's title bar) will reveal additional categories. Explore!!!

Watchers

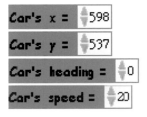

Watchers (simple and detailed) can be found in an object's viewer by clicking on the small menu to the left of its property. A watcher can be added to a project to track a particular property of an object. Detailed watchers are shown here. A "simple" watcher shows only the numeric value.

World

The World is the basis or foundation of any Squeak project. Simulations can run directly in the world. While the default color of the world is gray, it can be changed to your liking (by choosing the gray "repaint" handle).

The following is a small selection of books written by thinkers of "powerful ideas" whose names have been mentioned in this book or whose work has had significant influence on our curriculum development and practice.

Jerome S. Bruner. *Toward a Theory of Instruction.* Harvard University Press, 1974.

Alan Cromer. *Uncommon Sense: The Heretical Nature of Science.* Oxford University Press, New York, 1993.

Stillman Drake. *Galileo at Work: His Scientific Biography.* University of Chicago Press, 1981.

Yasmin Kafai and Mitchel Resnick (editors). *Constructionism in Practice: Designing, Thinking and Learning in a Digital World.* Lawrence Erlbaum Associates, 1996.

Alan C. Kay. *A Personal Computer for Children of All Ages.* Xerox Palo Alto Research Center, August 1972.

Alan C. Kay. *Computers, Networks and Education.* Scientific American, September 1991. http://www.squeakland.org/school/HTML/sci_amer_article/sci_amer_01.html

Maria Montessori. *The Secret of Childhood.* Ballantine Books, 1992.

Philip and Phylis Morrison. *The Ring of Truth: an inquiry into how we know what we know.* Random House, Inc., 1987. ISBN 0–394–55663–1.

Pat Murphy, Ellen Klages and Linda Shore. *The Science Explorer: An Exploratorium-at-Home Book.* The Exploratorium, San Francisco, CA, 2003.

Seymour Papert. *Mindstorms: Children, Computers and Powerful Ideas.* Basic Books, New York, 1980.

Seymour Papert. *Situating Constuctionism.* In I. Harel and S. Papert (editors). *Constructionism.* Ablex Publishing, Norwood, New Jersey, 1991.

Jean Piaget and Barbel Inhelder. *The Psychology of the Child.* Basic Books, New York, 2000.

Jean Piaget. *The Child's Conception of Number.* Norton Press, New York, 1965.

Mitchel Resnick. *Xylophones, Hamsters and Fireworks: The Role of Diversity in Constructionist Activities.* In I. Harel and S. Papert (editors). *Constructionism.* Ablex Publishing, Norwood, New Jersey, 1991.

Mitchel Resnick. *Turtles, Termites and Traffic Jams: Explorations in Massively Parallel Microworlds.* MIT Press, Cambridge, Massachusetts, 1994.

R. P. Taylor (editor). *The Computer in the School: Tutor, Tool, Tutee.* Teachers College Press, New York, 1980.

If you would like a more technical treatment of these ideas then the following two works are a great starting point.

H. Abelson and A. diSessa. *Turtle Geomety: The Computer as a Medium for Exploring Mathematics.* MIT Press, Cambridge, Massachusetts, 1980.

Michael Travers. *Agar: An Animal Construction Kit.* Master's Thesis, MIT, 1988. http://xenia.media.mit.edu/~mt/agar/agar.html

The authors wish to give a deep bow of acknowledgement and thanks to our friend and colleague Peter Maguire. Peter is the talented artist who breathed life into "Adam Link," the character who has appeared on the pages of this book and joined us through our Etoy adventures. Peter took painstaking effort to ensure that each of the graphics we chose for this book would appear crisp and clean in its final form.

We also give a multitude of thanks to Ian Piumarta, our editor and the brains behind the final typesetting and formatting of this book. We are so grateful for Ian's volunteer efforts toward this most laborious task.

Final thanks to our colleagues — the teachers and friends that proofread and "beta-tested" the projects in this book, and for the comments and encouragement they provided along the way.

BJ & Kim

BJ Conn has been a teacher in the Los Angeles Unified School District for 36 years and is currently teaching at the Open Charter School. She has been working for the last 20 years to create meaningful ways to help integrate technology into classroom curricula, especially in the areas of math and science. She is the recipient of numerous grants and awards for her work, and was nominated for Teacher of the Year in 1988. BJ has been called upon to share her knowledge and successes with technology within the Los Angeles Unified School District, as well as numerous conferences and workshops throughout the United States.

BJ has had the pleasure of working with Alan Kay since 1985, when the Open Charter School was chosen to be the research site for Apple Computer's Vivarium Project.

BJ received her Bachelor of Arts Degree from California State College at Los Angeles in 1968. She has worked as a teacher consultant for Apple Computer and Walt Disney Imagineering Research & Development. She is also a member of the International Academy of Digital Arts & Sciences.

Kim Rose is co-founder and Executive Director of Viewpoints Research Institute, Inc., a non-profit organization devoted to the continued development of Squeak and other new media environments. She is also a Systems Program Manager at Hewlett-Packard. A media developer, media critic, and cognitive scientist, she has worked with Alan Kay and his team since 1986.

Kim works with children and teachers in a variety of schools, universities, and community learning centers around the world to develop and test Squeak and Squeak-based collaborative dynamic curricula, and to explore how powerful ideas can become more accessible to children.

Kim received her Bachelor of Arts Degree from the University of California, Los Angeles (UCLA) in 1979. In 1995 she was a visiting scholar at NYU's Media Ecology Department. In 2000, Prentice Hall published a book edited by Kim and Mark Guzdial entitled "Squeak Open Personal Computing and Multimedia."

Kim has known BJ Conn for over 17 years and has spent many, many hours collaborating with BJ inside and outside the classroom.